Classic Tales

Level 2

# King Arthur and the Sword

*Retold by Rachel Bladon*
*Illustrated by Andy Catling*

##  Contents

| | |
|---|---|
| *King Arthur and the Sword* | 2 |
| Exercises | 20 |
| Picture Dictionary | 22 |
| About *Classic Tales* | 24 |

**OXFORD**

UNIVERSITY PRESS

Uther is the king of England. He is a good king. He and his queen have a beautiful baby boy.

2

But England is not a safe place. There are many bad men, and they want to be king. The boy cannot live in the castle, because it is not safe.

One day the king says to the queen, 'Sir Ector is a good man. He is a good knight. Our boy can live with Sir Ector and his son.'

So the king says to his servant, 'Take my boy to Sir Ector. But do not say, "This is the king's son." Tell nobody.'

The king's servant takes the boy to Sir Ector's house. Sir Ector is a good father to him, and his son Kay is a good brother.

The boy, Arthur, is soon big and strong. He is the king's son, but he does not know it. He loves Sir Ector, and he loves Sir Ector's son Kay.

Sometimes Sir Ector takes the boys to a tournament. They like to see the beautiful horses, and the strong knights.

'I want to fight in tournaments,' says Kay, 'when I'm older.'

I want to fight in tournaments.

King Uther is dead.

One day a servant comes to Sir Ector's house.

'King Uther is dead,' the servant says.

Sir Ector falls to his knees, and he cries for the king of England.

'Come tomorrow to the big stone on the road to London,' says the servant. 'All the king's knights must go there.'

So, the next day, Sir Ector goes to the big stone on the road to London. Merlin and all the knights of England are there.

Merlin is a good man. He is a friend of the kings of England, and he knows many things.

There is a sword in the stone. It is a beautiful sword, with jewels on it.

'Only the king of England can take this sword out of the stone!' Merlin says. 'Who wants to try?'

One knight comes to the stone. He pulls and he pulls, but the sword doesn't move.

Then another knight tries, and another. But nobody can take the sword out of the stone.

I can take the
sword out.

Every day, men come to the
big stone on the road to London.

'I am a good, strong man,' each
one says. 'I can take the sword out,
and be king of England.'

Everyone tries, but nobody can take the
sword out. And so England has no king.

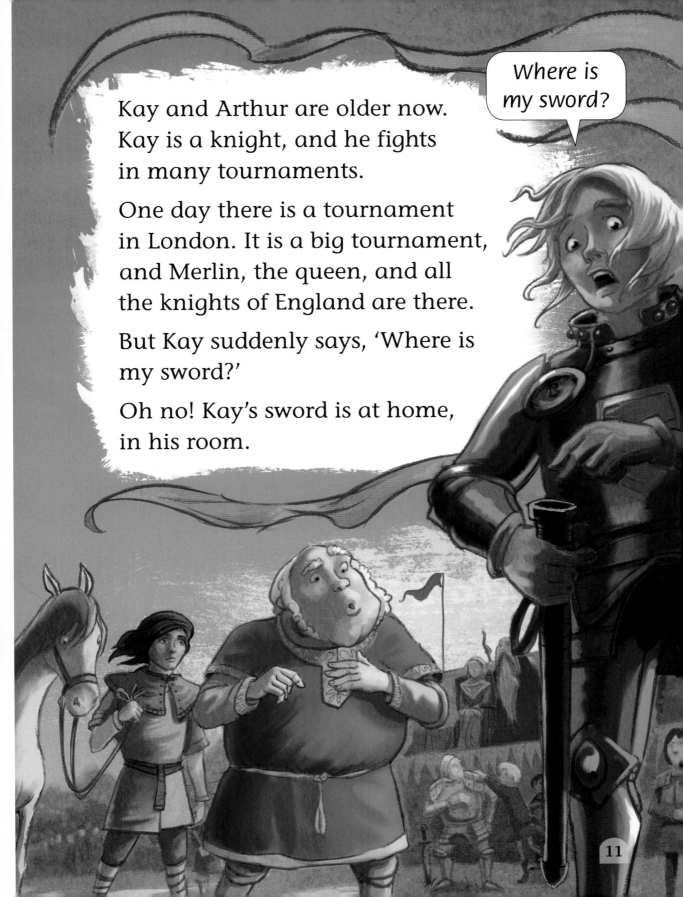

Kay and Arthur are older now. Kay is a knight, and he fights in many tournaments.

One day there is a tournament in London. It is a big tournament, and Merlin, the queen, and all the knights of England are there.

But Kay suddenly says, 'Where is my sword?'

Oh no! Kay's sword is at home, in his room.

*Where is my sword?*

'I can ride home, Kay,' says Arthur. 'I can ride home fast, and get your sword!'

He starts to ride home very fast. But on the road, he sees a big stone. There is a sword in the stone. A beautiful sword, with jewels on it.

'Kay can fight with this sword,' Arthur thinks. 'Then I can put it back after the tournament.'

Arthur pulls the sword, and it comes out of the stone. Then he rides to the tournament.

Arthur takes the sword to Kay and says, 'Here's a sword, Kay! You can fight with this sword. Then I can put it back.'

But the people at the tournament all stop and look.

'It's the sword!' one person says. 'The sword from the stone! This boy is the king! He is the new king of England!'

Some of the people are angry.

'He is not the king!' they say.
'He's Sir Ector's boy!'

'Bring Merlin!' somebody
says. 'Bring Merlin!'

Come with us to the stone, boy.

Merlin sees the sword, and he says, 'Come with us to the stone, boy.'

So Merlin, Arthur, and all the people go to the big stone. Merlin puts the sword back in the stone.

'I want to try,' says one of the men.

He comes to the stone. He pulls the sword, but it doesn't move.

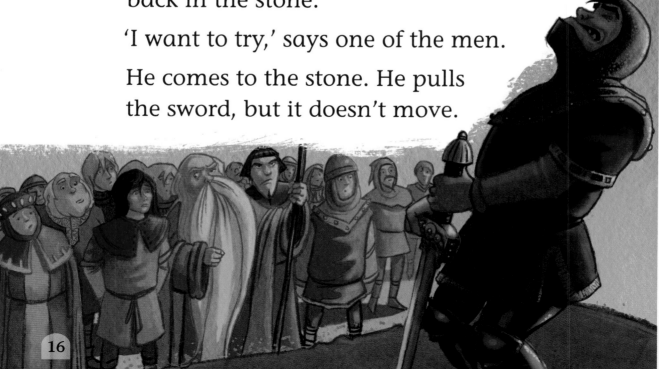

Another man tries, and another. But the sword doesn't move.

Then Merlin says to Arthur, 'Take the sword out of the stone, boy.'

Arthur goes to the stone. He pulls the sword ... and it comes out.

'He is the king!' the people say.

'I am not a king,' Arthur says.
'My father is Sir Ector.'

Now King Uther's servant comes to
Arthur and falls to his knees. 'Sir
Ector is not your father,' he says.
'You are the son of King Uther.'

'And now you are king of
England,' says Merlin.

'We have a king!' the people
say. 'England has a king!'

So from that day, Arthur is king of England. He lives in Uther's castle, with Merlin and his mother, and with Sir Ector and Kay.

Soon King Arthur has a beautiful queen, Guinevere. He is a good king and the people love him. And he always carries the beautiful sword – the sword from the stone.

# Exercises

## 1 Write the names.

Arthur   Kay   King Uther   ~~Sir Ector~~   Merlin   Guinevere

1 The servant takes King Uther's baby boy to __Sir Ector__ .

2 _____ wants to fight in tournaments when he's older.

3 _____ is a friend of the kings of England.

4 A servant tells Sir Ector, ' _____ is dead.'

5 _____ pulls the sword out of the stone.

6 England soon has a new queen, _____ .

## 2 Answer the questions.

1 Who's this? __It's Arthur.__

2 Can he pull the sword out of the stone? _____

3 Does he take the sword to Kay?
_____

4 Is he Sir Ector's son?
_____

5 Is he King Uther's son?
_____

6 Is he the new king of England? _____

# 3 Match and write the words.

safe ~~beautiful~~ strong bad baby big

**1**

a _beautiful_ horse

**2**

a _____ knight

**3**

a _____ boy

**4**

a _____ stone

**5**

a _____ place

**6**

a _____ man

# 4 Make sentences about the story. Then number them 1–5.

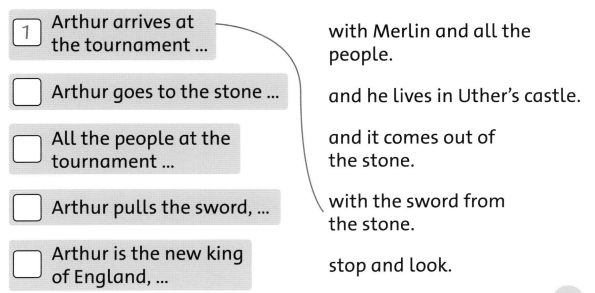

| 1 | Arthur arrives at the tournament ... | with Merlin and all the people. |
| | Arthur goes to the stone ... | and he lives in Uther's castle. |
| | All the people at the tournament ... | and it comes out of the stone. |
| | Arthur pulls the sword, ... | with the sword from the stone. |
| | Arthur is the new king of England, ... | stop and look. |

# Picture Dictionary

castle

come out

cry

dead *He is dead.*

fight

horses

jewels

king

knees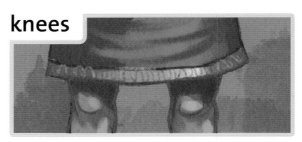

knight

**pull**

**put back**

**queen**

**ride**

**road**

**safe** *She's safe.*

**servant**

**stone**

**strong** *He is strong.*

**sword**

**take out**

**tournament**

# Classic Tales

Classic stories retold for learners of English – bringing the magic of traditional storytelling to the language classroom

For Classic Tales Teacher's Handbook, visit www.oup.com/elt/readers/classictales

### Level 1: 100 headwords
- The Enormous Turnip
- The Lazy Grasshopper
- The Little Red Hen
- Lownu Mends the Sky
- The Magic Cooking Pot
- The Magpie and the Milk
- Mansour and the Donkey
- Peach Boy
- The Princess and the Pea
- Rumpelstiltskin
- The Shoemaker and the Elves
- Three Billy-Goats

### Level 2: 150 headwords
- Amrita and the Trees
- Big Baby Finn
- The Fisherman and his Wife
- The Gingerbread Man
- Jack and the Beanstalk
- King Arthur and the Sword
- Rainforest Boy
- Thumbelina
- The Town Mouse and the Country Mouse
- The Ugly Duckling

### Level 3: 200 headwords
- Aladdin
- Bambi and the Prince of the Forest
- Goldilocks and the Three Bears
- The Heron and the Hummingbird
- The Little Mermaid
- Little Red Riding Hood
- Rapunzel

### Level 4: 300 headwords
- Cinderella
- Don Quixote: Adventures of a Spanish Knight
- The Goose Girl
- Sleeping Beauty
- The Twelve Dancing Princesses

### Level 5: 400 headwords
- Beauty and the Beast
- The Magic Brocade
- Pinocchio
- Snow White and the Seven Dwarfs

## OXFORD
UNIVERSITY PRESS

Great Clarendon Street, Oxford, OX2 6DP, United Kingdom

Oxford University Press is a department of the University of Oxford. It furthers the University's objective of excellence in research, scholarship, and education by publishing worldwide. Oxford is a registered trade mark of Oxford University Press in the UK and in certain other countries

© Oxford University Press 2015

The moral rights of the author have been asserted

First published in 2015

2020  2019

10 9 8 7 6

ISBN: 978 0 19 423989 9        Book
ISBN: 978 0 19 410819 5        e-Book
ISBN: 978 0 19 423995 0        Activity Book and Play
ISBN: 978 0 19 401430 4        Audio Pack

Printed in China

This book is printed on paper from certified and well-managed sources

ACKNOWLEDGEMENTS
Illustrations by: Andy Catling/Advocate Art